Dear Gemma,
Happy Birthday in Australia!
Love from
Den, Lisa, Nick & Alex
xxxx

Brisbane

a panoramic gift book

Steve Parish

Contents

Brisbane

from the heart

Queensland is the second largest Australian State, and has more than three million people who enjoy an abundance of blessings. Blue skies, white fluffy clouds, winter warmth, aqua-blue seas, lush forested ranges, a profusion of wildlife; in all, "beautiful one day, and perfect the next". That is Queensland in a nutshell, particularly the south-east corner, which the majority of Queensland's population calls home.

Having lived in most of Australia's capital cities I feel more than qualified to say that Brisbane is, without doubt, Australia's most livable capital city. The fecundity of the climate and soil are greatly underrated benefits — when you plant something, it grows!

Having now lived in Brisbane for 27 years, all the while recording its features on film, I am pleased to have been able to create this book to share the joys of Brisbane.

Steve Parish

River City

where it all began...

In 1824 a convict settlement was established on the banks of the Brisbane River. This began Brisbane's 35-year transformation from Yuggera tribal land to capital of the British colony of Queensland. As free settlers took up holdings around Brisbane Town, the more adventurous headed west to grazing land. By the 1860s Brisbane had become a thriving port for South-East Queensland's wool and wheat industries. Over the next 100 years its fortunes were linked to the cycles of primary production and mining. Economic prosperity has seen Brisbane shake off its country-town image — now it is a modern city. As technology, commerce and tourism take it into the 21st century, I think that the subtropical touch will keep Brisbane's charm alive.

The winding Brisbane River creates a relaxing lifestyle for locals — even in the heart of the city centre.

Since its opening in 1940, the Story Bridge has linked Kangaroo Point and Petrie Bight, connecting Brisbane's eastern suburbs with the city and Fortitude Valley.

Pages 10–11: The view of Brisbane's skyline from Mt Gravatt.

Lights decorating the Story Bridge illuminate the Brisbane River in a glorious spectrum of colour.

Looking south-east from Central Station over
Anzac Square and Post Office Square.

Brisbane City Hall, built between 1920 and 1930,
sits elegantly beside King George Square.

The passing parade in Queen Street Mall, the city's hub.

A Compact City

small, neat and rich with delights

Brisbane's central business district is contained by a small grid of streets named after colonial-era British royalty. I think the public squares, arcades and tree-shaded streets make it user-friendly — it can be crossed in about 20 minutes. The city's retail hub is the Queen Street Mall; the shopping and entertainment are on offer seven days a week.

Fortitude Valley predates Queen Street as Brisbane's retail centre. In the 1860s it was where local farmers set up a produce market. A fledgling Chinatown soon followed, and has grown into one of the Valley's main attractions. The weekend retro markets and a lively café and club scene are also drawcards.

Out & About

the outdoors beckon

A cosmopolitan population gives Brisbane a whole world of cuisines; they all use local produce, fresh seafood and seasonal tropical fruits. Paddington, West End, Milton, New Farm and Stones Corner are all lively spots close to the city. The riverfront restaurants usually have the bonus of great city views.

The Saturday markets in Brunswick Street, the Valley.

Cafés in Park Road, Milton — a great strip for fine dining.

Heritage buildings at the river end of Edward Street in the city.

Top: Chinatown is a colourful place to visit.
Above: Eager shoppers embrace the South Bank Lifestyle Market.

The Riverside Centre is the hub of Brisbane's financial precinct.

A variety of nightclubs, bistros and restaurants cater to all tastes at Eagle Street Pier.

Paddlewheelers and ferries operate from Eagle Street Pier, offering idyllic ways to tour the Brisbane River.

Left to right: Participants in a historical re-enactment at the George Street Heritage Festival; revellers at the festival take a ride in a brewer's dray.

History Captured

step back in time

Brisbane takes pride in its architectural heritage. You can bring to life the story of Brisbane's evolution by taking a self-guiding walk through the inner city — an array of architectural styles records Brisbane's changing needs and prosperity. The Shrine of Remembrance, Naldham House and the Port Office are fine examples of the popular Classic Revival style, while the Georgian simplicity of the convict-built Commissariat Stores on William Street stands in striking contrast to the French Renaissance facade of nearby Old Parliament House.

Above: The convict-built Old Mill, Wickham Terrace.
Right: The Regatta Hotel, Toowong.

Close-up of an entrance to The Mansions, George Street.

The stately entrance to Parliament House, George Street.

The beautiful Customs House on Queen Street —
restored and run by the University of Queensland.

The Mansions buildings on George Street were built during the Victorian era in 1889.

The Queen Street frontage of the Treasury Casino, which is an outstanding example of Italian Renaissance architecture.

The city, the tightly bent river, the Story Bridge and Kangaroo Point, with the towers and marina of Dockside on the right, and New Farm across the river on the far right.

Dockside and its yacht moorings.

Kangaroo Point

a prime riverside area

Kangaroo Point is one of many pockets of land created by the Brisbane River's looping course. Home owners and apartment dwellers seek out its river and city views. Picnic facilities and an award-winning boardwalk run along the base of the cliffs — a favourite spot for rock climbing. Dockside apartments, restaurants and a marina form a bustling complex on the river's Shafston Reach.

Sculptures at the base of the Kangaroo Point cliffs.

A climber scales the cliffs at Kangaroo Point.

The lagoon at South Bank Parklands is the centre of an oasis just 10 minutes walk from Queen Street and the heart of Brisbane's CBD.

In sunny weather, Brisbanites flock to South Bank.

South Bank

picturesque parklands

Since hosting World Expo 1988, South Bank has evolved into a 16-hectare oasis of leisure and cultural pursuits set against the backdrop of the city centre. Lush gardens set the scene for relaxation, and South Bank is a great place for a family outing that has something for everyone. The riverside promenade, palm-fringed lagoon and market stalls attract thousands of visitors on weekends. Outdoor movies, concerts, fireworks displays and the passing parade provide year-round entertainment. The riverside restaurants and cafés offer good food and wonderful city views.

Visitors stroll beneath South Bank's award-winning steel arbour, which is covered in luscious bougainvillia.

When the temperature rises, South Bank Lagoon is a favourite place to cool down and swim.

The main entrance to the Queensland Art Gallery.

State Library of Queensland — a stylish, informative public edifice.

Theatrical performances to enthral audiences both young and old are on offer at the Queensland Performing Arts Complex.

Gallery of Modern Art.

Cultural Heart

exceptional exhibits & entertainment

At the Queensland Cultural Centre in South Brisbane, I enjoy browsing through the exhibitions and permanent collections of the State's art gallery, museum and library. This splendid centre is also home to the concert hall and theatres of the Performing Arts Complex. Nearby is the Brisbane Convention and Exhibition Centre, which holds more than 400 events each year.

Powerhouse

a premier venue for the live arts

The Brisbane Powerhouse Centre for the Live Arts at New Farm is an industrial building transformed. The former power station and surrounds make a wonderful performance space, and the Powerhouse's program is contemporary and innovative.

Watermark by Richard Tipping in the Powerhouse forecourt.

Top and above: Aerial shots of the Powerhouse precinct.

UQ

a place of learning

Although established in 1909, the University of Queensland did not move to the St Lucia site until 1948. The Great Court, a ring of handsome sandstone buildings, forms the hub of this 110-hectare campus.

Above: University of Queensland campus from the air.
Above right: The entrance to one of the sandstone buildings.

Branching wooden stairs, ornate wooden finials on corrugated iron roofs, deep verandahs and iron lace — Queenslanders cover the hillsides close to the city.

Queenslander

practical housing, signature style

Brisbane's signature housing style is known as the "Queenslander". Designed to lessen the effects of cyclones, floods, termites and humid summers, these timber houses sit high above the ground on tin-capped hardwood stumps. Deep verandahs and high-pitched roofs, traditionally red or green, help keep them cool inside. These practical houses perch precariously on city ridges to catch prevailing breezes, whimsically embellished with elaborate trimmings of white timber or wrought iron. Proud owners lovingly restore them, while builders of new houses try to replicate them. To me, Queenslanders are the essence of Brisbane.

Parks & Gardens

glorious greenery

Brisbane's reputation as a livable city stems partly from its public gardens. The 16 hectares of the City Botanic Gardens include broad lawns, multi-hued flower beds and outstanding specimen trees.

Downriver, New Farm Park is famous for its rose gardens and splendid avenue of jacarandas. An obstacle course in the aerial roots of some huge fig trees fascinates most children that I know.

The Mt Coot-tha Botanic Gardens, just 8 kilometres from the CBD, form a 52-hectare living museum displaying Australian and exotic plants in rainforest, arid, woodland and wetland habitats. Among its treasures are a scented garden that excites your nose and a Japanese garden that soothes your spirit.

Roma Street Parkland opened in 2001. The beautiful themed garden areas are a huge improvement on the old railway yards that used to stand on the site.

The lily pond at Mt Coot-tha is a wonderful place to while away an afternoon.

The Mangrove Boardwalk at the City Botanic Gardens shades walkers as they stroll.

When the jacaranda trees flower, Brisbane drifts in a haze of blue-mauve blossom. This avenue of jacarandas is in New Farm Park.

The lake at Roma Street Parkland is a wonderful spot to admire the surrounding greenery.

Roma Street Parkland (clockwise from top left): Wendy Mills' sculpture *Concentric Intersection* is a feature of the Spectacle Garden; the bridge across Fern Gully; sandstone sculptures by Rhyl Hinwood; stepping stones in the Lake Precinct.

Inside the geodesic dome that houses a wonderland of tropical plants at the Mt Coot-tha Botanic Gardens.

The City Botanic Gardens from the air. On the left is the city campus of the Queensland University of Technology. On the right are moorings used by visiting yachts.

The view of the city and surrounding suburbs east from Mt Coot-tha.

Mt Coot-tha

the lookout

A scenic drive winds up Mt Coot-tha to reveal a remarkable panorama. The view sweeps around from the peaks of the Border Ranges in the south, across the city to Moreton Bay and northwards to the Glass House Mountains, then north-west over the D'Aguilar Range.

Above right: Visitors at the Mt Coot-tha Lookout enjoying the view.

Wild Places

animal refuges

D'Aguilar National Park stretches north from the Mt Coot-tha Lookout along the D'Aguilar Range. It takes in areas of eucalypt forest, woodland and subtropical rainforest. This outstanding national park, divided into two sections, provides outdoor recreation facilities important to Brisbane's people.

The wildlife from the ranges spills down into Brisbane's lush urban spread, and there are many species of birds, frogs, mammals, reptiles and insects that live and thrive in the suburbs. Two excellent places to observe native flora and fauna are the Redlands IndigiScapes Centre, which promotes indigenous plant species in a beautiful setting, and Daisy Hill Koala Centre, located within Daisy Hill Conservation Park in Brisbane's south-east.

D'Aguilar National Park has many quiet nooks where you can immerse yourself in natural beauty.

Clockwise from left: Friendly faces of the local inhabitants — Orange-eyed Tree-frog; Marbled Frogmouth; Wanderer Butterfly.

Rare Squirrel Gliders can be found in the eucalypt forest of southern Queensland.

The Common Brushtail Possum abounds in Brisbane.

Koalas live in D'Aguilar National Park and the conservation areas around Tingalpa Reservoir.

Colourful Rainbow Lorikeets decorate the city's surrounds and are commonly seen.

Early morning sun glistens on the northern end of North Stradbroke Island.

Stradbroke

idyllic islands

Stradbroke Island is now two, where once it was one. In 1896 a storm washed through a narrow neck of sand, dividing the island into North and South Stradbroke — North Stradbroke, called Minjerriba or "Giant in the sun" by the local Aboriginal people, is usually known just as "Straddie" to its population and the citizens of Brisbane.

Mineral sand and silica have been mined on Stradbroke for decades, and the island was one of the first sites where stringent rules for habitat restoration were set down. Other industries include fishing and oyster farming, but the island is mainly known for local tourism — most of us in Brisbane would prefer "Straddie" to stay our secret, as it is one of the most beautiful unsung island retreats in the world.

Moreton Island

sensational sand mass

Moreton Island is in the north of Moreton Bay on the seaward side. It was formed by sand washing up against Cape Moreton, a granite outcrop, and is part of the same sand mass that formed the Cooloola coast and Fraser, Bribie and Stradbroke Islands. The Port of Brisbane's main shipping channel lies close to the western shore of Moreton Island, and it looks like the huge container ships pass by within arm's reach of its bayside beaches.

Most of the island is now part of Moreton Island National Park, but the old whaling station at Tangalooma is a family resort. You can go there to enjoy the beauty and serenity of the forest, freshwater lakes, ocean and bay beaches, fishing, dune tobogganing or dolphin watching.

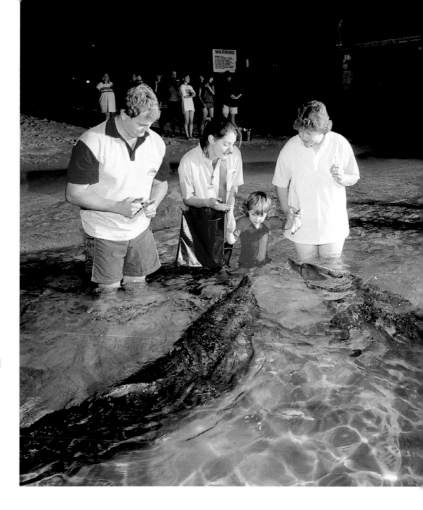

At night, bottlenose dolphins come in to Tangalooma to be fed and "chat" to fans.

Feather stars on coral — the reefs off Moreton are a diver's dream, rich in life and colour.

The golden beach fronts some equally golden skyscrapers, here looking south from The Spit at the Gold Coast.

The Gold Coast

beautiful, beckoning beaches

The Gold Coast, less than an hour's drive from Brisbane, is a mecca for holidaymakers. Its sheltered waterways and sun-drenched beaches stretch 50 kilometres south from Sanctuary Cove to Coolangatta. As well as sun, sand and surf, the Gold Coast has sophisticated international resorts and theme parks that children and teenagers love. It is a shopper's paradise; I find the array of retail venues staggering — it will tempt anyone, either buyer or browser. With its cafés, clubs, a casino and restaurants, the Gold Coast glitters on long after sunset.

Looking south over Sea World, towards Surfers Paradise.

South Nobby, looking south to Burleigh Heads.

Tweed Heads with Coolangatta beyond.

Currumbin Rock juts out to sea, protecting the mouth of Currumbin Creek.

A popular holiday destination since it was little more than sand dunes and shacks — looking south from Miami Beach.

Left to right: Purlingbrook Falls and Natural Bridge — both spectacular natural features of Springbrook National Park.

The Scenic Rim

the mountains behind

A wonderland of dramatic valleys and escarpments lies within The Scenic Rim, an arc of ranges stretching 300 kilometres on Brisbane's south-east. A series of national parks that includes Tamborine, Springbrook and Lamington showcases some of the world's few remaining stands of subtropical rainforest. Wildlife is plentiful and many animals show little fear of humans. This is outstanding country for bushwalking — along the woodland and forest trails are panoramic views as well as mountain creeks tumbling into pure, clear rock pools.

Cascading Chalahn Falls, Lamington National Park, South-East Queensland.

Sunshine Coast

north to the sun

Beyond Bribie Island lies the Sunshine Coast, a great place for holidays and weekend getaways. The superb beaches are intersected by scenic headlands and estuaries, and stretch from Caloundra to Noosa Heads. In the mountainous hinterland, small farms, charming towns and striking landscapes spread west from the coast to the Conondale and Jimna Ranges — an area known for its galleries, cottage industries, exotic crops and dairy products. The region is also the home of Australia Zoo, one of the country's great wildlife parks. The coastline continues northward from the mouth of the Noosa River along the Cooloola sand mass to Wide Bay, Tin Can Bay and Fraser Island. Fraser Island is a World Heritage Area of towering dunes, perched lakes and majestic forests, besides being the largest sand island in the world.

Top: The peaceful loveliness of Alexandria Bay, Noosa Heads National Park.
Above: An aerial shot of Noosa Heads National Park and beaches.

Twilight envelops a canoeist on Pumicestone Passage, between Bribie Island and the mainland, where the Glass House Mountains are silhouetted against the sky.

On Fraser Island, the world's largest sand island and a World Heritage Area, perched lakes lie in hollows between massive sand dunes.

Fraser Island

heavenly habitats

The battle between conservationists and those who wanted to extract Fraser's natural resources brought this magnificent sand island, the most extensive in the world, to everyone's attention. Largely due to the efforts of the admirable and determined John Sinclair, the island is now listed by the National Estate as a World Heritage National Park.

Fraser Island is 123 kilometres long and over 184,000 hectares in area. I love its superb beaches, its freshwater creeks running to the sea through stands of rainforest, the perched lakes filled with crystal-clear water, its heathlands vibrant with birds, and the wealth of wildlife.

Top and above: Young male Humpback Whales play and show off during their annual migration through Hervey Bay on their way up Australia's east coast.

From an early age, Steve Parish has been driven by his undying passion for Australia to photograph every aspect of it, from its wild animals and plants to its many wild places. Then he began to turn his camera on Australians and their ways of life. This body of work forms one of Australia's most diverse photographic libraries. Over the years, these images of Australia have been used in thousands of publications, from cards, calendars and stationery to books – pictorial, reference, guide and children's. Steve has combined his considerable talents as a photographer, writer, poet and public speaker with his acute sense of needs in the marketplace to create a publishing company that today is recognised worldwide.

Steve's primary goal is to turn the world on to nature, and, in pursuit of this lifelong objective, he has published a world-class range of children's books and learning aids. He sees our children as the decision makers of tomorrow and the guardians of our heritage.

Published by Steve Parish Publishing Pty Ltd
PO Box 1058, Archerfield, Queensland 4108 Australia

© copyright Steve Parish Publishing Pty Ltd
All rights reserved.

ISBN 9781174021087 4

First published 2001. Reprinted 2005, 2006, 2007, 2009, 2011.

Photography: Steve Parish

Additional photography: Front cover and pp. 5, 6–7, 12–13, 1 4 (right), 27-28 & 38, Emma Harm; pp. 1, 10–11, 17 (top right), 30 (bottom), 31 & 42, Greg Harm

Design: Gill Stack
Editing: Ted Lewis; Michele Perry, Karin Cox, SPP
Production: Tiffany Johnson

Front cover: The city and Story Bridge in evening regalia. Inset: A glorious stretch of sand at the Gold Coast. Title page: Brisbane River curves around City Botanic Gardens, with the CBD gleaming beyond. Page 62–3: Boats moored in front of the Riverside Centre.

Printed in China through Phoenix Offset

Produced in Australia at the Steve Parish Publishing Studios

Steve Parish
PUBLISHING

PROUDLY AUSTRALIAN OWNED

www.steveparish.com.au